Colors: Green

Esther Sarfatti

Rourke
Publishing LLC
Vero Beach, Florida 32964

www.rourkepublishing.com

PHOTO CREDITS: © Miroslav Ferkuniak: title page; © Viorika Prikhodko: page 3; © Don Bayley: page 5; © Olga Shelego: page 9; © Nico Smit: page 11; © Robert Churchill: page 17; © Denise Bentley: page 21; © Christine Balderas, Denis Sauvageau, Robert Dodge: page 23.

Editor: Robert Stengard-Olliges

Cover design by Nicola Stratford, bdpublishing.com

Library of Congress Cataloging-in-Publication Data

Sarfatti, Esther.
  Colors : green / Esther Sarfatti.
    p. cm. -- (Concepts)
  ISBN 978-1-60044-518-7 (Hardcover)
  ISBN 978-1-60044-659-7 (Softcover)
  1. Colors--Juvenile literature. 2. Green--Juvenile literature. I. Title.
  QC495.5.S356 2008
  535.6--dc22

                                    2007014028

Rourke Publishing
Printed in the United States of America, North Mankato, Minnesota
081810
081710LP-A

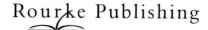

Rourke Publishing

www.rourkepublishing.com – rourke@rourkepublishing.com
Post Office Box 3328, Vero Beach, FL 32964

This page is green.

Green is my favorite color.

I like green trees.

I like green grapes.

9

I like green frogs.

I like green snakes.

13

I like green lizards.

I like green watermelons.

I like green grass.

I like green clovers.

So many things are green.
Do you like green, too?

23

Index

Further Reading

Anderson, Moira. *Finding Colors: Green*. Heinemann, 2005.

Schuette, Sarah L. *Green: Seeing Green All Around Us*. Capstone Press, 2006.

Recommended Websites

www.enchantedlearning.com/colors/green.shtml

About the Author

Esther Sarfatti has worked with children's books for over 15 years as an editor and translator. This is her first series as an author. Born in Brooklyn, New York, and brought up in a trilingual home, Esther currently lives with her husband and son in Madrid, Spain.